Do Your Best Every Day!

The Ultimate Daily Planner

Activinotes

Activinotes

DAILY JOURNALS, PLANNERS, NOTEBOOKS AND OTHER BLANK BOOKS

I0669580

THE ULTIMATE DAILY PLANNER

DATE

	TIME

TO DO LIST:

- ☐
- ☐
- ☐
- ☐
- ☐
- ☐
- ☐
- ☐
- ☐
- ☐

AGENDA	TIME

NOTES:

THE ULTIMATE DAILY PLANNER

DATE

	TIME

TO DO LIST:

- ☐
- ☐
- ☐
- ☐
- ☐
- ☐
- ☐
- ☐
- ☐

AGENDA	TIME

NOTES:

THE ULTIMATE DAILY PLANNER

DATE

TO DO LIST:

	TIME

AGENDA	TIME

NOTES:

THE ULTIMATE DAILY PLANNER

DATE

	TIME

TO DO LIST:

- ☐
- ☐
- ☐
- ☐
- ☐
- ☐
- ☐
- ☐
- ☐

AGENDA	TIME

NOTES:

THE ULTIMATE DAILY PLANNER

DATE

TO DO LIST:

	TIME

AGENDA	TIME

NOTES:

THE ULTIMATE DAILY PLANNER

DATE

TO DO LIST:

	TIME

AGENDA	TIME

NOTES:

THE ULTIMATE DAILY PLANNER

DATE

	TIME

TO DO LIST:

- [ ]
- [ ]
- [ ]
- [ ]
- [ ]
- [ ]
- [ ]
- [ ]
- [ ]

AGENDA	TIME

NOTES:

THE ULTIMATE DAILY PLANNER

DATE

	TIME

TO DO LIST:

- ☐
- ☐
- ☐
- ☐
- ☐
- ☐
- ☐
- ☐
- ☐

AGENDA	TIME

NOTES:

THE ULTIMATE DAILY PLANNER

DATE

TO DO LIST:

	TIME

NOTES:

AGENDA	TIME

THE ULTIMATE DAILY PLANNER

DATE

TO DO LIST:

	TIME

AGENDA | **TIME**

NOTES:

THE ULTIMATE DAILY PLANNER

DATE

TIME

TO DO LIST:

AGENDA | **TIME**

NOTES:

THE ULTIMATE DAILY PLANNER

DATE

TO DO LIST:

	TIME

AGENDA	TIME

NOTES:

THE ULTIMATE DAILY PLANNER

DATE

	TIME

TO DO LIST:

- [ ]
- [ ]
- [ ]
- [ ]
- [ ]
- [ ]
- [ ]
- [ ]
- [ ]

AGENDA	TIME

NOTES:

THE ULTIMATE DAILY PLANNER

DATE

	TIME

TO DO LIST:

- ☐
- ☐
- ☐
- ☐
- ☐
- ☐
- ☐
- ☐
- ☐

AGENDA	TIME

NOTES:

THE ULTIMATE DAILY PLANNER

DATE

	TIME

TO DO LIST:

- ☐
- ☐
- ☐
- ☐
- ☐
- ☐
- ☐
- ☐
- ☐

AGENDA	TIME

NOTES:

THE ULTIMATE DAILY PLANNER

DATE

TO DO LIST:

TIME

AGENDA | **TIME**

NOTES:

THE ULTIMATE DAILY PLANNER

DATE

	TIME

TO DO LIST:

- ☐
- ☐
- ☐
- ☐
- ☐
- ☐
- ☐
- ☐
- ☐

NOTES:

AGENDA	TIME

THE ULTIMATE DAILY PLANNER

DATE

TO DO LIST:

	TIME

AGENDA	TIME

NOTES:

THE ULTIMATE DAILY PLANNER

DATE

TO DO LIST:

	TIME

AGENDA | **TIME**

NOTES:

THE ULTIMATE DAILY PLANNER

DATE

TIME

TO DO LIST:

AGENDA | **TIME**

NOTES:

THE ULTIMATE DAILY PLANNER

DATE

TO DO LIST:

	TIME

AGENDA | **TIME**

NOTES:

THE ULTIMATE DAILY PLANNER

DATE

	TIME

TO DO LIST:

	TIME

AGENDA | **TIME**

NOTES:

THE ULTIMATE DAILY PLANNER

DATE

	TIME

TO DO LIST:

- ☐
- ☐
- ☐
- ☐
- ☐
- ☐
- ☐
- ☐
- ☐

AGENDA	TIME

NOTES:

THE ULTIMATE DAILY PLANNER

DATE

TO DO LIST:

	TIME

AGENDA	TIME

NOTES:

THE ULTIMATE DAILY PLANNER

DATE

TIME

TO DO LIST:

AGENDA **TIME**

NOTES:

THE ULTIMATE DAILY PLANNER

DATE

	TIME

TO DO LIST:

☐
☐
☐
☐
☐
☐
☐
☐
☐

AGENDA	TIME

NOTES:

THE ULTIMATE DAILY PLANNER

DATE

TO DO LIST:

	TIME

AGENDA	TIME

NOTES:

THE ULTIMATE DAILY PLANNER

DATE

TO DO LIST:

	TIME

AGENDA

	TIME

NOTES:

THE ULTIMATE DAILY PLANNER

DATE

TIME

TO DO LIST:

AGENDA | **TIME**

NOTES:

THE ULTIMATE DAILY PLANNER

DATE

TO DO LIST:

	TIME

AGENDA

	TIME

NOTES:

THE ULTIMATE DAILY PLANNER

DATE

TIME

TO DO LIST:

AGENDA

TIME

NOTES:

THE ULTIMATE DAILY PLANNER

DATE

TIME

TO DO LIST:

AGENDA | **TIME**

NOTES:

THE ULTIMATE DAILY PLANNER

DATE

TO DO LIST:

	TIME

AGENDA	TIME

NOTES:

THE ULTIMATE DAILY PLANNER

DATE

TO DO LIST:

	TIME

AGENDA	TIME

NOTES:

THE ULTIMATE DAILY PLANNER

DATE

	TIME

TO DO LIST:

- ☐
- ☐
- ☐
- ☐
- ☐
- ☐
- ☐
- ☐
- ☐

AGENDA	TIME

NOTES:

THE ULTIMATE DAILY PLANNER

DATE

TO DO LIST:

TIME

AGENDA | **TIME**

NOTES:

THE ULTIMATE DAILY PLANNER

DATE

TO DO LIST:

	TIME

AGENDA	TIME

NOTES:

THE ULTIMATE DAILY PLANNER

DATE

	TIME

TO DO LIST:

- [ ]
- [ ]
- [ ]
- [ ]
- [ ]
- [ ]
- [ ]
- [ ]
- [ ]

AGENDA	TIME

NOTES:

THE ULTIMATE DAILY PLANNER

DATE

TO DO LIST:

	TIME

AGENDA	TIME

NOTES:

THE ULTIMATE DAILY PLANNER

DATE

TO DO LIST:

	TIME

NOTES:

AGENDA	TIME

THE ULTIMATE DAILY PLANNER

DATE

TIME

TO DO LIST:

AGENDA | **TIME**

NOTES:

THE ULTIMATE DAILY PLANNER

DATE

TO DO LIST:

	TIME

AGENDA | **TIME**

NOTES:

THE ULTIMATE DAILY PLANNER

DATE

	TIME

TO DO LIST:

- ▢
- ▢
- ▢
- ▢
- ▢
- ▢
- ▢
- ▢
- ▢

AGENDA	TIME

NOTES:

THE ULTIMATE DAILY PLANNER

DATE

TIME

TO DO LIST:

NOTES:

AGENDA | **TIME**

THE ULTIMATE DAILY PLANNER

DATE

TO DO LIST:

TIME

AGENDA **TIME**

NOTES:

THE ULTIMATE DAILY PLANNER

DATE

	TIME

TO DO LIST:

- ☐
- ☐
- ☐
- ☐
- ☐
- ☐
- ☐
- ☐
- ☐

AGENDA	TIME

NOTES:

THE ULTIMATE DAILY PLANNER

DATE

TO DO LIST:

	TIME

AGENDA | **TIME**

NOTES:

THE ULTIMATE DAILY PLANNER

DATE

TO DO LIST:

	TIME

AGENDA	TIME

NOTES:

THE ULTIMATE DAILY PLANNER

DATE

	TIME

TO DO LIST:

- [ ] _____
- [ ] _____
- [ ] _____
- [ ] _____
- [ ] _____
- [ ] _____
- [ ] _____
- [ ] _____
- [ ] _____

AGENDA	TIME

NOTES:

THE ULTIMATE DAILY PLANNER

DATE

TO DO LIST:

	TIME

AGENDA	TIME

NOTES:

THE ULTIMATE DAILY PLANNER

DATE

TIME

TO DO LIST:

AGENDA | **TIME**

NOTES:

THE ULTIMATE DAILY PLANNER

DATE

	TIME

TO DO LIST:

- ☐
- ☐
- ☐
- ☐
- ☐
- ☐
- ☐
- ☐
- ☐

AGENDA	TIME

NOTES:

THE ULTIMATE DAILY PLANNER

DATE

	TIME

TO DO LIST:

- ☐
- ☐
- ☐
- ☐
- ☐
- ☐
- ☐
- ☐
- ☐

NOTES:

AGENDA	TIME

THE ULTIMATE DAILY PLANNER

DATE

TIME

TO DO LIST:

AGENDA **TIME**

NOTES:

THE ULTIMATE DAILY PLANNER

DATE

TIME

TO DO LIST:

AGENDA | **TIME**

NOTES:

THE ULTIMATE DAILY PLANNER

DATE

TO DO LIST:

	TIME

AGENDA	TIME

NOTES:

THE ULTIMATE DAILY PLANNER

DATE

TO DO LIST:

	TIME

AGENDA	TIME

NOTES:

THE ULTIMATE DAILY PLANNER

DATE

TO DO LIST:

	TIME

NOTES:

AGENDA	TIME

THE ULTIMATE DAILY PLANNER

DATE

	TIME

TO DO LIST:

- [ ]
- [ ]
- [ ]
- [ ]
- [ ]
- [ ]
- [ ]
- [ ]
- [ ]

AGENDA	TIME

NOTES:

THE ULTIMATE DAILY PLANNER

DATE

TO DO LIST:

	TIME

AGENDA

	TIME

NOTES:

THE ULTIMATE DAILY PLANNER

DATE

	TIME

TO DO LIST:

- [ ]
- [ ]
- [ ]
- [ ]
- [ ]
- [ ]
- [ ]
- [ ]
- [ ]

AGENDA	TIME

NOTES:

THE ULTIMATE DAILY PLANNER

DATE

	TIME

TO DO LIST:

- ☐
- ☐
- ☐
- ☐
- ☐
- ☐
- ☐
- ☐

AGENDA	TIME

NOTES:

THE ULTIMATE DAILY PLANNER

DATE

TO DO LIST:

	TIME

AGENDA	TIME

NOTES:

THE ULTIMATE DAILY PLANNER

DATE – – – – – –

	TIME

TO DO LIST:

- ☐
- ☐
- ☐
- ☐
- ☐
- ☐
- ☐
- ☐

AGENDA	TIME

NOTES:

THE ULTIMATE DAILY PLANNER

DATE

TIME

TO DO LIST:

AGENDA | **TIME**

NOTES:

THE ULTIMATE DAILY PLANNER

DATE

TIME

TO DO LIST:

AGENDA | **TIME**

NOTES:

THE ULTIMATE DAILY PLANNER

DATE

TO DO LIST:

	TIME

AGENDA	TIME

NOTES:

THE ULTIMATE DAILY PLANNER

DATE

TO DO LIST:

	TIME

AGENDA	TIME

NOTES:

THE ULTIMATE DAILY PLANNER

DATE

TIME

TO DO LIST:

AGENDA | **TIME**

NOTES:

THE ULTIMATE DAILY PLANNER

DATE

TIME

TO DO LIST:

AGENDA **TIME**

NOTES:

THE ULTIMATE DAILY PLANNER

DATE

TO DO LIST:

	TIME

AGENDA | **TIME**

NOTES:

THE ULTIMATE DAILY PLANNER

DATE

TIME

TO DO LIST:

AGENDA | **TIME**

NOTES:

THE ULTIMATE DAILY PLANNER

DATE

TO DO LIST:

	TIME

AGENDA | **TIME**

NOTES:

THE ULTIMATE DAILY PLANNER

DATE

TIME

TO DO LIST:

AGENDA | **TIME**

NOTES:

THE ULTIMATE DAILY PLANNER

DATE

	TIME

TO DO LIST:

- ☐
- ☐
- ☐
- ☐
- ☐
- ☐
- ☐
- ☐
- ☐

AGENDA	TIME

NOTES:

THE ULTIMATE DAILY PLANNER

DATE

TIME

TO DO LIST:

AGENDA **TIME**

NOTES:

THE ULTIMATE DAILY PLANNER

DATE

TO DO LIST:

	TIME

AGENDA	TIME

NOTES:

THE ULTIMATE DAILY PLANNER

DATE

	TIME

TO DO LIST:

- [ ]
- [ ]
- [ ]
- [ ]
- [ ]
- [ ]
- [ ]
- [ ]
- [ ]

AGENDA	TIME

NOTES:

THE ULTIMATE DAILY PLANNER

DATE

TO DO LIST:

TIME

AGENDA | **TIME**

NOTES:

THE ULTIMATE DAILY PLANNER

DATE

	TIME

TO DO LIST:

- ☐
- ☐
- ☐
- ☐
- ☐
- ☐
- ☐
- ☐
- ☐

AGENDA	TIME

NOTES:

THE ULTIMATE DAILY PLANNER

DATE

	TIME

TO DO LIST:

- [ ]
- [ ]
- [ ]
- [ ]
- [ ]
- [ ]
- [ ]
- [ ]
- [ ]

AGENDA	TIME

NOTES:

THE ULTIMATE DAILY PLANNER

DATE

TO DO LIST:

	TIME

AGENDA	TIME

NOTES:

THE ULTIMATE DAILY PLANNER

DATE

TIME

TO DO LIST:

AGENDA **TIME**

NOTES:

THE ULTIMATE DAILY PLANNER

DATE

TO DO LIST:

	TIME

AGENDA

	TIME

NOTES:

THE ULTIMATE DAILY PLANNER

DATE

TO DO LIST:

	TIME

AGENDA	TIME

NOTES:

THE ULTIMATE DAILY PLANNER

DATE

TO DO LIST:

TIME

AGENDA | **TIME**

NOTES:

THE ULTIMATE DAILY PLANNER

DATE

TO DO LIST:

	TIME

AGENDA	TIME

NOTES:

THE ULTIMATE DAILY PLANNER

DATE

TIME

TO DO LIST:

AGENDA

TIME

NOTES:

THE ULTIMATE DAILY PLANNER

DATE

TO DO LIST:

	TIME

NOTES:

AGENDA	TIME

THE ULTIMATE DAILY PLANNER

DATE

TO DO LIST:

	TIME

AGENDA

	TIME

NOTES:

THE ULTIMATE DAILY PLANNER

DATE

TO DO LIST:

TIME

AGENDA | **TIME**

NOTES:

THE ULTIMATE DAILY PLANNER

DATE

	TIME

TO DO LIST:

- ☐
- ☐
- ☐
- ☐
- ☐
- ☐
- ☐
- ☐
- ☐

AGENDA	TIME

NOTES:

THE ULTIMATE DAILY PLANNER

DATE

TO DO LIST:

TIME

AGENDA

TIME

NOTES:

THE ULTIMATE DAILY PLANNER

DATE

	TIME

TO DO LIST:

☐
☐
☐
☐
☐
☐
☐
☐
☐

AGENDA | **TIME**

NOTES:

THE ULTIMATE DAILY PLANNER

DATE

TIME

TO DO LIST:

AGENDA   **TIME**

NOTES:

THE ULTIMATE DAILY PLANNER

DATE

TO DO LIST:

	TIME

AGENDA	TIME

NOTES:

THE ULTIMATE DAILY PLANNER

DATE

TO DO LIST:

	TIME

AGENDA	TIME

NOTES:

THE ULTIMATE DAILY PLANNER

DATE

	TIME

TO DO LIST:

AGENDA	TIME

NOTES:

THE ULTIMATE DAILY PLANNER

DATE

	TIME

TO DO LIST:

- [ ]
- [ ]
- [ ]
- [ ]
- [ ]
- [ ]
- [ ]
- [ ]
- [ ]

AGENDA	TIME

NOTES:

THE ULTIMATE DAILY PLANNER

DATE

TO DO LIST:

	TIME

AGENDA	TIME

NOTES:

THE ULTIMATE DAILY PLANNER

DATE

TIME

TO DO LIST:

AGENDA | **TIME**

NOTES:

THE ULTIMATE DAILY PLANNER

DATE

TO DO LIST:

	TIME

NOTES:

AGENDA	TIME

THE ULTIMATE DAILY PLANNER

DATE

	TIME

TO DO LIST:

- [ ] _____
- [ ] _____
- [ ] _____
- [ ] _____
- [ ] _____
- [ ] _____
- [ ] _____
- [ ] _____
- [ ] _____

NOTES:

AGENDA	TIME

THE ULTIMATE DAILY PLANNER

DATE

	TIME

TO DO LIST:

- [ ]
- [ ]
- [ ]
- [ ]
- [ ]
- [ ]
- [ ]
- [ ]
- [ ]

AGENDA	TIME

NOTES: